The

and

Disorder

Act 1998

Fergus Smith

B.Sc(Hons), M.A., C.Q.S.W.,D.M.S., Dip.M

in consultation with

Paul Carr

M.A.(Cantab)
District Judge (Magistrates'Courts)

Children Act Enterprises Ltd (CAE)
103 Mayfield Road
South Croydon
Surrey CR2 0BH

www.caeuk.org

© Fergus Smith

British Library Cataloguing in Publication Data
A catalogue record for this book is available from the
British Library

ISBN 1 899986 91 X

Designed and typeset by Andrew Haig & Associates
Printed in the UK by The Lavenham Press

All rights reserved. Except as permitted under the
Copyright, Designs and Patents Act 1988, this
publication may not be reproduced, stored in a retrieval
system, or transmitted in any form or by any means,
without the prior written permission of the publisher.

CAE is an independent organisation which publishes
guides to family and criminal law and provides
consultancy, research, training and independent
investigation services to the public, private and voluntary
sectors.

*No part of this publication may be reproduced without
the written consent of the authors*

Contents

Abbreviations

ASBA 2003 = Anti-social Behaviour Act 2003

ATCSA 2001 = Anti-terrorism, Crime and Security Act 2001

CA 1989 = Children Act 1989

CDA 1971 = Criminal Damage Act 1971

CDA 1998 = Crime and Disorder Act 1998

CJA 1991 = Criminal Justice Act 1991

CJA 2003 = Criminal Justice Act 2003

CJCSA 2000 = Criminal Justice and Court Services Act 2000

CJPA 2001 = Criminal Justice and Police Act 2001

CJPOA 1994 = Criminal Justice and Public Order Act 1994

CSA 1997 = Crime (Sentences) Act 1997

CYPA 1933 = Children and Young Persons Act 1933

CYPA 1969 = Children and Young Persons Act 1969

EA 1996 = Education Act 1996

MHA 1983 = Mental Health Act 1983

PACE 1984 = Police and Criminal Evidence Act 1984

PCCSA 2000 = Powers of Criminal Courts (Sentencing) Act 2000

PHA 1997 = Protection from Harassment Act 1997

POA 1986 = Public Order Act 1986

PRA 2002 = Police Reform Act 2002

YJCEA 1999 = Youth Justice and Criminal Evidence Act 1999

Introduction

- This guide has been written for all those in England and Wales who are involved in the system of criminal justice in so far as it relates to children and young persons.

- It provides a succinct, accessible and accurate summary of relevant provisions of the Crime and Disorder Act 1998 updated to reflect the amendments introduced by the Criminal Justice Act 2003 and the Anti-social Behaviour Act 2003.

- The guide should be used only to supplement not replace the Act itself, or official Home Office guidance.

Key Points of the CDA 1998

- The Act's principal aim is to prevent offending so as to create safer communities.

- Multi-agency partnerships are critical to the reduction of offending amongst children and young people.

- Local authorities and other public agencies must consider the crime and disorder implications of all their decisions.

- Certain 'racially or religiously aggravated' crimes require their seriousness to be marked. Specific offences carry enhanced penalties and sentences are increased generally for racially aggravated offences.

Concepts & Principles (alphabetical order)

Abolition of Presumption of 'Doli Incapax' [s.34 CDA 1998]

- The rebuttable presumption that a child is incapable of telling the difference between serious wrong and simple naughtiness is abolished.

- For purposes of criminal law a child who has reached the age of criminal responsibility i.e. a 10–13 years old will be treated in the same way as a young person of 14–17 years of age when deciding whether or not s/he has the capacity to commit a criminal offence.

Action Plan Orders [s.69 PCCSA 2000]

- Are short intensive programmes of community-based intervention combining punishment, rehabilitation and reparation.

Child Safety Orders [s.11 CDA 1998]

- The aim of this Order is to protect those aged under 10 who are at risk of becoming involved in crime, and may require a child to be at home at certain times or to stay away from certain places or people and be under the supervision of a 'responsible officer' of the local authority or YOT.

Child's Silence at Trial [s.35 CDA 1998] s.35

■ CJPOA 1994 which allowed a court to draw inferences from the failure of the accused (aged 14 or over) to give evidence or answer questions at trial is extended and applies to all persons aged 10 or over.

Final Warning Schemes [s.65 CDA 1998]

■ Repeat cautioning is abolished and replaced with a statutory police reprimand and final warning scheme, with any further offence resulting in prosecution.

Parenting Orders [s.8 CDA 1998]

■ Aim to support parents to control the behaviour of their children and will require parents to attend counselling/guidance sessions.

Racially or Religiously Aggravated Offences [ss.28–32 CDA 1998 as amended by s.39 ATCSA 2001 & s.153 PCCSA 2000]

■ The Act introduces new offences of racially or religiously aggravated assault, criminal damage, harassment and public order offences with significantly higher maximum penalties.

■ Where it can be shown that they were racially or religiously aggravated, courts must treat all other offences as more serious.

Referral Order [s.16 PCCSA 2003]

▣ A compulsory or discretionary referral by a court of a youth offender to a multi-disciplinary panel.

Reparation Orders [s.73 PCCSA 2000]

▣ Reparation Orders are intended to make young offenders face up to the consequences of their actions and might involve a personal or written apology or repairing criminal damage.

Time Limits [s.44 CDA 1998]

▣ The Act introduces statutory time limits for young offenders for the periods between arrest and first listing and between conviction and sentence.

▣ The Prosecution of Offences (Youth Courts Time Limits) Regulations 1999 which gave effect to Parliament's intentions in the above respect have been revoked. Thus, although the above provision remains, no regulations currently exist.

Youth Offending Teams (YOTs) [s.39 CDA 1998]

▣ Mandatory multi-agency teams involving social workers, probation and police officers as well as health and education staff who must deliver community-based intervention programmes to make young persons address their offending behaviour.

Youth Justice Board [s.41 CDA 1998]

- A non-Departmental public body, sponsored by the Home Office to oversee youth justice services in England and Wales.

Prevention of Crime & Disorder
& General Provisions

Responsibilities of Local Authorities Police & Others [ss.5–7 & 17 CDA 1998 as amended]

- Local authorities (London boroughs/county councils/ unitary authorities), chief officer/s of police for the area within those authorities, PCTs and fire authorities are 'responsible authorities' and jointly responsible for working together to reduce local crime and disorder and combat misuse of drugs in their area [s.5 (1) CDA 1998 as amended by s.97 (2) PRA 2002].

  NB. s.97 PRA 2002 is in force with effect from 30.04.04.

- In so doing, the responsible authorities are obliged to co-operate with:
  - Every police authority any part of whose area lies within the area in question
  - Every local probation board or health authority primary care trust any part of whose area lies within the area in question and
  - Any individual or agencies prescribed by the Secretary of State

- The above organisations and individuals must co-operate with the responsible authorities in their exercise of their functions [s.5(2) CDA 1998]

  NB. Responsible authorities must also invite participation of individuals or organisations which the Secretary of State may order [s.5 (3) CDA 1998].

Formulation & Implementation of Strategies [s.6 CDA 1998]

■ Responsible authorities are required to formulate and implement for the period to September 30 2001 (and thereafter every 3 years) a strategy for the reduction of crime and disorder and for combating the misuse of drugs in their area [s.6 (1) & (7) CDA 1998].

■ Before formulating the strategy, the responsible authorities must:
- Review levels and patterns of crime and disorder and of the level and pattern of misuse of drugs in their in the area (taking due account of the knowledge and experience of local people)
- Analyse the results
- Publish in the area a report of that analysis and
- Obtain, via public meetings or otherwise the views of relevant agencies and individuals (including any identified in a s.5(3) Order made by the Secretary of State) [s.6(2) CDA 1998]

■ Taking account of the analysis and views obtained from relevant agencies and individuals, responsible authorities must formulate a strategy to include:
- Objectives agreed amongst identified stakeholders
- Long and short-term performance targets [s.6(3)&(4) CDA 1998]

- Having formulated their strategy, responsible authorities must publish in their area a report which includes details of:

  - Co-operating persons and agencies
  - The published analysis of their review of local crime and disorder and misuse of drugs
  - The agreed strategy, including in particular objectives, who is responsible for their attainment and performance targets [s.6(5) CDA 1998]

- While implementing a strategy the responsible authorities must keep it under review so as to monitor its effectiveness and make any changes which appear necessary or expedient [s.6 (6) CDA 1998].

  NB. Responsible authorities must submit annual and such other reports as s/he may require, to the Secretary of State on work done locally [s.7 (1) & (2) CDA 1998. the Secretary of State also has powers under s.6(6A) to require strategies on specified crimes and disorder.

  In Wales, the focus is 'substance misuse (i.e. alcohol as well as other drugs) and reports are presented to the Secretary of State and the Welsh Assembly.

Duty to Consider Crime & Disorder Implications [s.17 CDA 1998]

- All local authorities including joint authorities, police authorities, national parks, London's fire and emergency planning authority and the 'broads authorities' must in carrying out any of their functions have due regard to likely effect of, and do all they reasonably can to prevent crime and disorder.

Youth Justice System

Aim of Youth Justice System [s.37 CDA 1998]

- The principal aim is to prevent offending by children and young persons [s.37 (1) CDA 1998].

- In addition to any other duty they may have, all individuals and agencies carrying out functions in relation to the youth justice system must have regard to that aim [s.37 (2) CDA 1998].

Local Provision of Youth Justice Services [s.38 CDA 1998 as amended by Sch.4 para.28 YJCEA 1999, Sch.9 para.197 PCCSA 2000 & s.29(2) ASBA 2003]

- Local authorities acting in co-operation with police, local probation boards and health authorities/primary care trusts must ensure that, to such extent as is appropriate for their area, all youth justice services are available [s.38 (1) CDA 1998].

- Chief officers of police authorities, local probation boards and health authorities/primary care trusts must co-operate in the local authority's discharge of its duty [s.38(2) CDA 1998]

- All the above parties are empowered to contribute toward expenditure incurred in provision of youth justice services by:
  - Direct payments or
  - Contributing to a fund established and

maintained by the local authority out of which payments may be made [s.38(3) CDA 1998]

- Youth justice services are currently defined as:
  - Provision of persons to act as appropriate adults to safeguard the interests of children and young persons detained or questioned by police
  - Assessment of children/young persons and provision of rehabilitation programmes associated with s.66(2) CDA 1998 final warnings
  - Bail support for those remanded or committed on bail while awaiting trial or sentence
  - Placement in local authority accommodation of those remanded or committed under s.23 CYPA 1969
  - Provision of reports or other information required by courts in criminal proceedings against children/young persons
  - Performance of YOTs of functions under ss.25–27 ASBA 2003
  - Provision of persons to act as responsible officers in relation to Parenting Orders, Child Safety Orders, Reparation Orders and Action Plan Orders
  - Supervision of young persons sentenced to a Community Rehabilitation Order, Community Punishment Order or a Community Rehabilitation and Punishment Order [renamed by Schedule7 CJCSA 2000]

- Supervision of children/young persons sentenced to a Detention and Training or Supervision Order
- Post-release supervision of children/young persons under s.37(4A) or s.65 CJA 1991 or s.31 CSA 1997
- Performance of functions under s.102 PCCSA 2000 (period of detention and training under Detention and Training Order) by such persons as may be authorised by Secretary of State [s.38(4) CDA 1998]
- The implementation of Referral Orders within the meaning of the PCCSA 2000

Youth Offending Teams (YOTs)

Duty to Provide YOTs [s.39 (1) & (3) CDA 1998]

▪ Each local authority acting in co-operation with chief officers of police and relevant local probation boards, health authorities/primary care trusts must establish for their area one or more YOTs.

NB. 2 or more local authorities acting together may establish one or more YOTs for both (or all) their areas [s.39(2) CDA 1998]

▪ The local authority and individuals and agencies referred to above are empowered to make payments towards expenditure incurred by, or for purposes connected with YOTs by:
  - Making payments directly or
  - Contributing to a fund, established and maintained by the local authority out of which the payments may be made [s.39(4)]

Membership of YOTs

▪ A YOT must, [s.39(5)CDA 1998], include at least one of each of the following:
  - A probation officer
  - A social worker of a local authority
  - A police officer
  - A person nominated by a health authority/primary care trust, any part of whose area lies within the local authority area
  - A person nominated by the chief education officer

■ A YOT may also include such other persons as the local authority thinks appropriate having consulted its partners [s.39 (6) CDA 1998].

Purpose of YOTs

■ Duties of YOTs are to:
- Co-ordinate provision of youth justice services for all those in the authority's area who need them
- Carry out such functions as are assigned to team in youth justice plan formulated under s.40(1) CDA 1998 (see below) [s.39(7) CDA 1998]

Youth Justice Plans [s.40 CDA 1998]

■ Each local authority must after consultation with relevant persons and bodies, formulate and implement an annual plan which sets out how:
- Youth justice services will be provided and funded
- YOT/s established by them (alone or jointly) will be composed and funded and what their functions will be [s.40(1) CDA 1998]

NB. Relevant persons and bodies are those cited in s.38 CDA 1998 and include, where the local authority is a county council, any district council whose districts form part of the area [s.40 (2) CDA 1998].

- Functions assigned to YOTs may include in particular, para.7 (b) Sch.2 CA 1989 (local authority's duty to take reasonable steps to encourage children not to commit offences [s.40 (3) CDA 1998].

- A local authority must submit its youth justice plan to the Youth Justice Board and must publish it in such a manner and by such a date as the Secretary of State may direct [s.40 (4) CDA 1998].

Youth Justice Board [s.41 CDA 1998]

Structure & Function of Board

■ There must be a Youth Justice Board for England and Wales which will be a non-departmental public body [s.41 (1); (2) CDA 1998].

■ The Board must consist of 10, 11 or 12 members appointed by Secretary of State including persons who have extensive recent experience of the youth justice system [s.41(3);(4) CDA 1998].

■ The functions of the Board are to:
  • Monitor the operation of the youth justice system and the provision of services
  • Advise Secretary of State on operation and provision of youth justice service, how its principal aim might be most effectively pursued, content of any national standards established, custodial accommodation and the steps that might be taken to prevent offending
  • Monitor the extent to which the principal aim is being achieved and any such standards met
  • Obtain information from relevant authorities so as to fulfil the above 3 functions
  • Publish information obtained from relevant authorities, identify, make known and promote good practice in operation and provision of youth justice services, prevention of offending

and work with young offenders or those at risk of offending

- Make grants, with the approval of the Secretary of State to local authorities/other bodies for them to develop such practice or to commission research in connection with such practice
- Commission research of the sort referred to above
- Enter into agreements for provision of accommodation for detaining persons subject to Detention and Training Orders, accommodating persons detained under ss. 90 and 91 PCCSA 2000, remanded to secure accommodation or remanding 17 year olds to custody
- Facilitate arrangements between the Secretary of State and any person providing such accommodation
- Offer assistance to local authorities in discussing their duty under s.61 CJA 1991 (provision of secure accommodation)
- Assess annually demand for secure remands and sentenced places and prepare a plan for Secretary of State on plans for exercise of functions with regard to secure estate [s.41(5) CDA 1998 as amended by the Youth Justice Board for England and Wales Order 2000 SI 2000/1160]

Other Provisions Relating to the Board

▨ The Secretary of State is empowered to add to or amend the functions of the Board [s.41 (6) CDA 1998] who must comply with the directions or guidance given by her/him [s.41 (7) CDA 1998].

▨ A relevant authority (i.e. local authority, chief officer of police, a police authority, a local probation board and a health authority/primary care trust [s.41(10 CDA 1998]) is obliged:
  - To provide the Board with any information they require to undertake the first three functions listed above and
  - Whenever so required, must provide the Board with a report (format of which may also be specified) of those of their youth justice activities specified by the Board [s.41(8) CDA 1998]

NB. The Board may arrange or require the above relevant authority to arrange for the report to be published in a manner considered by the Board to be appropriate [s.41 (9) CDA 1998].

Details of appointments to the Board, time limits for service, remuneration, operational procedures, annual reports etc are laid out in Sch.2 CDA 1998.

Racially or Religiously Aggravated Offences [ss.28–32 CDA 1998 amended by s.39 ATCSA 2001 & s.153 PCCSA 2000]

'Racially or Religiously Aggravated Offence'

- Racially or religiously aggravated for purposes of ss.29–32 CDA 1998 and s.153 PCCSA 2000 is if:
  - At time of committing it, or immediately before or after doing so, the offender demonstrates towards victim, hostility based on her/his actual or presumed (by offender) membership of racial or religious group or
  - Offence is wholly or partly motivated by hostility towards members of a racial or religious group based on their membership of that group [s.28(1) & (2) CDA 1998]

  NB. It is immaterial if hostility is also based to any extent on any other factor not mentioned above [s.28 (3). A racial group = persons defined by reference to race, colour, nationality (including citizenship) or ethnic or national origins [s.28 (4). A religious group = persons defined by religious beliefs or lack of religious belief [s.28 (5).

Racially or Religiously Aggravated Assaults [s.29 CDA 1998]

- A person is guilty of an offence under s.29 if s/he commits any of the following which are racially or religiously aggravated as defined in s.28 CDA 1998:
  - An offence under s.20 of Offences Against the Person Act 1861 (malicious wounding or grievous bodily harm)
  - An offence under s.47 of that Act (actual bodily harm) or
  - Common assault

- A person guilty of either of the first two is liable:
  - On summary conviction, to imprisonment for up to 6 months, or to a fine not exceeding the statutory maximum, or to both
  - On conviction on indictment, to imprisonment for up to 7 years, a fine, or both [s.29(2) CDA 1998]

- A person guilty of common assault is liable:
  - On summary conviction to imprisonment for up to 6 months, a fine not exceeding the statutory maximum, or both
  - On conviction on indictment, to imprisonment for up to 2 years, a fine, or both [s.29(3) CDA 1998]

Racially or Religiously Aggravated Criminal Damage [s.30 CDA 1998]

■ A person is guilty of an offence under s.30 (1) CDA 1998 if s/he commits:
- An offence under s.1(1) Criminal Damage Act 1971 (destroying or damaging property belonging to another) which is racially or religiously motivated as defined in s.28 CDA 1998

■ A person guilty of an offence under s.30 is liable:
- On summary conviction, to prison for up to 6 months, a fine not exceeding the statutory maximum, or both
- On conviction on indictment, to imprisonment for up to 14 years, a fine, or both [s.30(2) CDA 1998]

Racially or Religiously Aggravated Public Order Offences [s.31 CDA 1998]

■ A person is guilty of an offence under s.31(1)CDA 1998 if s/he commits an offence which is racially or religiously aggravated under:
- s.4 Public Order Act 1986 (fear or provocation of violence)
- s.4A of that Act (intentional harassment, alarm or distress) or
- s.5 of that Act (harassment, alarm or distress)

▪ A constable may arrest without warrant anyone who s/he reasonably suspects to be committing an offence under the first two of the above s.31 (1) provisions [s.31 (2) CDA 1998].

▪ A constable may arrest a person without warrant if:
  • S/he engages in conduct which a constable reasonably suspects to constitute an offence falling within the third of the above provisions and
  • S/he is warned by that constable to stop, yet engages in further such conduct immediately or shortly after the warning [s.31(3) CDA 1998]

  NB. The initial misconduct and the further conduct referred to need not be of the same nature.

▪ A person guilty of an offence within the 'fear or provocation of violence' or 'intentional harassment, alarm or distress' categories of s.31(1) is liable:
  • On summary conviction, to prison for up to 6 months, a fine not exceeding statutory maximum, or to both
  • On conviction on indictment, to prison for up to 2 years, or a fine, or to both [s.31(4) CDA 1998]

▪ A person guilty of an offence falling within the 'harassment, alarm or distress' provision of s.31(1) is liable :
  • On summary conviction, to a fine not exceeding level 4 on the standard scale [s.31(5) CDA 1998]

Racially or Religiously Aggravated Harassment [s.32 CDA 1998]

- A person is guilty of an offence under s.32(1) CDA 1998 if s/he commits a racially or religiously aggravated offence under:
    - s.2 (offence of harassment) or s.4 (putting people in fear of violence) of Protection from Harassment Act 1997

- A person guilty of an offence falling within the 'offence of harassment' provision above is liable:
    - On summary conviction, to imprisonment for up to 6 months or to fine not exceeding the statutory maximum, or to both;
    - On conviction on indictment, to imprisonment for a term of up to 2 years or to a fine, or to both [s.32 (3) CDA 1998].

- A person guilty of an offence falling within the 'putting people in fear of violence' provision is liable:
    - On summary conviction, to prison for up to 6 months or a fine not exceeding the statutory maximum, or both;
    - On conviction on indictment, to imprisonment for up to 7 years or to a fine or to both [s.32 (4) CDA 1998].

NB. If, on the trial on indictment of a person charged with racially or religiously aggravated harassment, the jury find her/him not guilty, they may find the person guilty of the basic offence of harassment. Similarly, a defendant found not guilty of racially or religiously aggravated putting people in fear of violence, may be found guilty of racially or religiously aggravated harassment [s.32(5) & (6) CDA 1998].

Seriousness of Other Racially or Religiously Aggravated Offences [s.153 PCCSA 2000 as amended by s.39 (7) ATCSA 2001]

- If a court is considering an offence other than one under ss.29–32 described above, which it believes to be racially or religiously aggravated, it must consider that this increases the seriousness of the offence, state in open court that it was so aggravated, and sentence accordingly.

Preventive Orders & Measures

Anti-Social Behaviour Orders [s.1; 1A CDA 1998]

■ An application for an order under this section may be made by a relevant authority i.e. the council for a local government area, (in England) County Council, any chief officer of police for the area, chief constable of British Transport Police Force, housing action trust or any person registered as a social landlord if it appears to them that the conditions described below are fulfilled with respect to any person aged 10 or over [s.1(1A) CDA 1998 as amended by s.61(1) PRA 2002]

NB. The Secretary of State now has the power to enable non-Home Office police forces to apply for Anti-Social Behaviour Orders [s.1A as inserted by s.62 PRA 2002].

Conditions [s.1 (1) (a) & (b) CDA 1998 as amended by s.61 (2) PRA 2002]

■ The conditions are that:
   • The person has, since the section's commencement on 01.04.99 [SI 1998/3263] acted in an anti-social manner i.e. a manner that caused or was likely to cause harassment, alarm or distress to one or more persons not of the same household as her/himself **and**
   • Such an order is necessary to protect relevant persons in the local government area in which

the harassment, alarm or distress was caused or was likely to be caused; in the police area or area policed by the British Transport police, or premises provided or managed by the social landlord, from further anti-social acts by her/him.

- Such an application must be made by complaint to the magistrates' court whose commission area includes the local government or police area concerned [s.1 (3) CDA 1998 as amended by s.61(6) PRA 2002].

- If on application, it is proved that the conditions mentioned in s.1 (1) are fulfilled the magistrates' court may make an 'Anti-Social Behaviour Order' under this section [s.1 (4) CDA 1998].

  NB. For the purposes of determining whether the 'anti-social manner' criterion of s.1 (1) (a) is satisfied the court must disregard any act of the defendant which s/he shows was reasonable in the circumstances [s.1 (5) CDA 1998].

  s.1B CDA 1998 introduced by s.63 PRA 2002 enables relevant authorities to apply to the County Court in certain circumstances for an Anti-Social Behaviour Order.

Effect of Anti-Social Behaviour Order [s.1 (4) & (6) as substituted by s.61 (7) PRA 2002]

- The above order prohibits the defendant from doing anything described in the order.

▨ Prohibitions are those necessary for the purpose of protecting from further anti-social acts by defendant, relevant persons elsewhere in England and Wales.

Consultation Requirements [s.1E CDA 1998 as inserted by s.66 PRA 2002]

▨ A council of a local government area must consult the chief officer of police with jurisdiction in that area before applying for an Anti-Social Behaviour Order.

▨ Similarly, a chief officer of police must consult the council of the local government area before s/he initiates an application.

▨ British Transport police and registered social landlords must consult both council and police.

Interim Orders [s.1D CDA 1998 as inserted by s.65 PRA 2002]

▨ A magistrates' court or the County Court are able to make an interim order under s.1 or new s.1B before the application process is complete, if the court considers it just to do so [s.1D(1) CDA 1998].

NB. Interim orders are not available to criminal courts because orders under s.1C (see below) can only be made in the criminal courts once the case is complete and the offender has been convicted.

Duration of Anti-Social Behaviour Order [s.1 (7) CDA 1998]

■ The order will have effect for a period not less than 2 years which is specified in the order, or until further order is made.

Variation or Discharge of Anti-Social Behaviour (including interim) Order [s.1 (8) & (9) CDA 1998]

■ Except by the consent of both parties, no Anti-Social Behaviour Order will be discharged before the end of the 2 years beginning with the date of service of the order [s.1 (9) CDA 1998].

   NB. The consent provision does not apply to an order under s.1C in criminal proceedings (see below).

■ The applicant or the defendant may apply by complaint to the court which made an Anti-Social Behaviour Order, for it to be varied or discharged by a further order [s.1 (8) CDA 1998] .

Breach of Anti-Social Behaviour (including interim) Order [s.1 (10) & (11) CDA 1998 as amended]

■ If, without reasonable excuse a person does anything which s/he is prohibited from doing by an Anti-Social Behaviour Order, s/he is guilty of an offence and liable:

- On summary conviction, to imprisonment for up to 6 months or a fine not exceeding the statutory maximum, or both;
- On conviction on indictment, to imprisonment for up to 5 years [s.1 (10)].

NB. A person convicted of such a breach cannot be given a conditional discharge under s.12 PCCSA 2000 [s.1 (11) CDA 1998].

Appeal against Anti-Social Behaviour (including interim) Order [s.4 CDA 1998]

- An appeal against an Anti-Social Behaviour Order made by the magistrates' court will be heard by the Crown Court.

- On such an appeal, the Crown Court:
  - May make such orders as may be necessary to give effect to its determination of the appeal and
  - May also make such incidental or consequential orders as appear to it to be just.

NB. Any order of the Crown Court made on an appeal under s.4 CDA 1998 (other than one directing an application be re-heard by the magistrates' court) must, for purposes of future variation or discharge applications be treated as if an order of the magistrates' court from which appeal was brought and not an order of the Crown Court.

Orders on Conviction in Criminal Proceedings [s.1C CDA 1998 as inserted by s.64 PRA 2002]

▪ Where a person has been convicted of a 'relevant offence' (i.e. an offence committed on or after 02.12.02) and the court considers an offender has acted, at any time since the commencement date, in an anti-social manner, and an order under this section is necessary to protect persons in England or Wales from further anti-social acts, it may make an order which prohibits the offender from doing anything described in that order [s.1C CDA 1998 inserted by s.64 PRA 2002 and amended by s.86 ASBA 2003].

NB. The court may make an order if the prosecutor asks it to do so or if the court thinks it appropriate. An order under this provision may be made only in addition to any sentence imposed [s.1C (4) CDA 1998]. An offender subject to an order under s.1C may apply to the court which made it for it to be varied or discharged.)

Individual Support Orders [s.1AA CDA 1998 introduced by s.322 CJA 2003]

Effect & Duration [s.1AA (1) & (2) CDA 1998]

- Where a court makes an Anti-Social Behaviour Order in respect of a defendant who is a child or young person when that order is made, it must consider whether the individual support conditions are fulfilled.

- If it is satisfied that those conditions are fulfilled, the court must make an order an 'Individual Support Order' which:
  - Requires the defendant to comply, for a period not exceeding 6 months, with such requirements as are specified in the order, and
  - Requires the defendant to comply with any directions given by the responsible officer with a view to the implementation of the above requirements

Condition for Making an Individual support Order [s.1AA (3) CDA 1998]

- The individual support conditions are that:
  - Such an order would be desirable in the interests of preventing any repetition of the kind of behaviour which led to the making of the Anti-Social Behaviour Order

- The defendant is not already subject to an Individual Support Order, and
- The court has been notified by the Secretary of State that arrangements for implementing Individual Support Orders are available in the area in which it appears to it that the defendant resides or will reside and the notice has not been withdrawn

- If the court is not satisfied that the individual support conditions are fulfilled, it shall state in open court that it is not so satisfied and why it is not [s.1AA(4) CDA 1998]

- The requirements that may be specified under s.1AA (2)(a) are those that the court considers desirable in the interests of preventing any repetition of the kind of behaviour which led to the making of the Anti-Social Behaviour Order.

Requirements of an Individual Support Order [s.1AA (6)–(7) CDA 1998]

- Requirements included in an Individual Support Order, or directions given under such an order by a responsible officer, may require the defendant to do all or any of the following things:
  - To participate in activities specified in the requirements or directions at a time or times so specified
  - To present her/himself to a person or persons so specified at a place or places and at a time or times so specified

- To comply with any arrangements for his education so specified [s.1AA(6) CDA 1998]

■ Requirements included in, or directions given under, such an order may not require the defendant to attend (whether at the same place or at different places) on more than 2 days in any week ('week' here means a period of 7 days beginning with a Sunday) [s.1AA(7) CDA 1998].

■ Requirements included in, and directions given under, an individual support order shall, as far as practicable, be such as to avoid:
- Any conflict with the defendant's religious beliefs; and
- Any interference with the times, if any, at which s/he normally works or attends school or any other educational establishment [s1AA(8) CDA 1998]

■ Before making an Individual Support Order, the court shall obtain from a social worker of a local authority social services department or a member of a YOT, and must consider, any information it considers necessary in order to determine:
- Whether the individual support conditions are fulfilled, or
- What requirements should be imposed by an Individual Support Order if made [s1AA(9) CDA 1998]

NB. A 'responsible officer' in relation to an Individual Support Order, means one of the following who is specified in the order: a social worker of a local authority social services department, a person nominated by a person appointed as chief education officer under s.532 of the Education Act 1996 or a member of a YOT.

- Before making an Individual Support Order, the court must explain to the defendant in ordinary language:
  - The effect of the order and of the requirements proposed to be included in it;
  - The consequences which may follow (under subsection (3) if s/he fails to comply with any of those requirements, and
  - That the court has power (under subsection (6) to review the order on the application either of the defendant or of the responsible officer [s.1AB(1) CDA 1998]

- If the person in respect of whom an Individual Support Order is made fails without reasonable excuse to comply with any requirement included in the order, s/he is guilty of an offence and liable on summary conviction to a fine not exceeding
  - If aged 14 or over at the date of conviction, £1,000
  - If aged under 14 then, £250 [s.1AB(3) CDA 1998]

- No referral order under section 16(2) or (3) of the Powers of Criminal Courts (Sentencing) Act 2000 (referral of young offenders to youth offender panels) may be made in respect of an offence under subsection (3) above.

- If the Anti-Social Behaviour Order as a result of which an Individual Support Order was made ceases to have effect, the Individual Support Order (if it has not previously ceased to have effect) also ceases to have effect [s.1AB (5) CDA 1998].

- On an application made by complaint by the person subject to an individual support order, or the responsible officer, the court which made the Individual Support Order may vary or discharge it by a further order [s.1AB (6) CDA 1998].

- If the Anti-Social Behaviour Order as a result of which an individual support order was made is varied, the court varying the anti-social behaviour order may by a further order vary or discharge the Individual Support Order [s.1AB (7) CDA 1998].

Parenting Orders [as amended by ASBA 2003]

■ A court must not make a Parenting Order unless it has been notified by the Secretary of State that arrangements for implementing them are available in the area where it appears to the court the parent resides/will reside and the notice had not been withdrawn [s.8 (3) CDA 1998]. A Home Office letter of 27.04.00 confirmed arrangements in place in all areas from 01.06.00.

Conditions [s.8 (1); (6) CDA 1998]

■ The court **may** impose a Parenting Order if, in any court proceedings:
  * A Child Safety Order is made in respect of a child
  * An Anti-Social Behaviour Order or Sexual Offences Prevention Order is made with respect to a child/young person
  * A child/young person is convicted of an offence or
  * A person is convicted of an offence under s.443 (failure to comply with School Attendance Order) or s.444 (failure to secure regular attendance at school of registered pupil) Education Act 1996

■ The relevant condition is that the Parenting Order would be desirable in the interests of preventing: (Where relevant) any repetition of the kind of behaviour which led to the Child Safety, Anti-Social or Sex Offender Order being made

- (Where relevant) the commission of any further offence by the child/young person
- (Where relevant) the commission of any further offence under s.443 or s.444 Education Act 1996

Effect of Parenting Order made under CDA 1998

- A Parenting Order requires the parent:
  - To comply, for a period of not more than 12 months with such requirements as are specified in the order and
  - To attend for a concurrent period not exceeding 3 months such counselling or guidance sessions as may be specified in directions given by the responsible officer [s.8(4) CDA 1998 as substituted by s.18 ASBA 2003]

  NB. If a Parenting Order has previously been made in respect of the parent, it may, but need not, include the requirements for counselling/guidance as described above [s.8 (5) CDA 1998].

- Requirements that may be specified in the order are those the court considers desirable in the interests of preventing any such repetition, or as the case may be, the commission of any such further offence [s.8 (7)].

- A counselling or guidance programme which a parent is required to attend by virtue of subsection

(4)(b) may be, or include a residential course **if** the court is satisfied that:

- The attendance of the parent is likely to more effective than her/his attendance at a non-residential course in preventing any such repetition or as the case may be, the commission of any such further offence and
- Any interference with family life which is likely to result from the attendance is proportionate [s.8(7A) CDA 1998 inserted by s.18 ASBA 2003]

- If an Anti Social Behaviour Order is made in respect of an under 16 year old, the court:
  - Must make a Parenting Order if satisfied that he relevant condition is satisfied
  - If it is not satisfied, must state in open court that it is not and why [s.9(1B) CDA 1998 inserted by s.85 ASBA 2003]

NB. The responsible officer for purposes of a Parenting Order is a probation officer, social worker of a local authority social services or YOT member (one of whom will be specified) [s.8(8) CDA 1998].

Procedural Requirements [s.9 CDA 1998 as amended]

- Where a person **under the age of 16** is convicted of an offence, the court which convicts her/him, unless prohibited from so doing because it has made a Referral Order **must**:
  - If it is satisfied that the relevant condition is fulfilled, make a Parenting Order and

- If not satisfied, state this and reasons in open court [s.9(1A) CDA 1998 inserted by Sch.4 para.27 YJCEA 1999 and amended by Sch.9 para. 195 PCCSA 2000]

NB. Court has discretion to consider making a Parenting Order in case of 16 or 17 year olds.

- In the following situations, before making a Parenting Order a court must obtain and consider information about the person's family circumstances and likely effect of the order on those circumstances:
  - A Child Safety Order is made
  - An under 16 year old convicted of an offence or made the subject of An Anti-Social Behaviour Order or Sexual Offences Prevention Order or
  - Is convicted of failure to comply with a School Attendance Order or to secure regular attendance at school where the person concerned is under 16. [s.9 (2) CDA 1998].

- Where a court proposes to make both a Referral Order and a Parenting Order it must first obtain and consider a report from an appropriate officer:
  - Indicating the requirements proposed by that officer to be included in the Parenting Order
  - Indicating the reasons why s/he considers those requirements desirable to prevent further offences
  - (in the case of an under 16 year old) containing information about her/his family circumstances and the likely effect of the order on those [s.9(2A) CDA 1998 inserted by Sch.34 CJA 2003]

■ Before making a Parenting Order, a court must explain to the parent in ordinary language:

- The effect of the order and of the requirements proposed to be included within it
- The consequences which may follow under subsection 7 (see below) if s/he fails to comply with any of those requirements and that
- The court has power (subsection 5) to review the order on the application either of the parent or of the responsible officer [s.9(3) CDA 1998]

NB. Requirements specified in, and directions given in a Parenting Order must, as far as practicable, avoid any conflict with a parent's religious beliefs and any interference with times, if any, at which s/he normally works or attends an educational establishment [s.9 (4) CDA 1998].

Variation and Discharge

■ If, while a Parenting Order is in force it appears to the court which made it, on the application of responsible officer or parent, that it is appropriate to do so, the court can vary or discharge the order by:

- Cancelling any provision included in it or
- Inserting in it (in addition to or instead of any existing provision) any provision that could have been included in the order if the court had then had power to make it and were exercising that power [s.9 (5) CDA 1998].

NB. Where an application to discharge is dismissed, no further application for its discharge can be made by any person except with the consent of the court which made the order [s.9 (6) CDA 1998].

Failure to Comply with Requirements [s.9 (7) CDA 1998]

■ If, while a Parenting Order is in force, the parent without reasonable excuse fails to comply with any requirement included in the order or specified in directions given by the responsible officer, s/he is liable on summary conviction to a fine not exceeding level 3 on the standard scale.

Appeals [s.10 CDA 1998]

■ With respect to Parenting Orders made by virtue of Child Safety Orders, appeals are to the High Court [s.10(1)(a) CDA 1998].

■ With respect to Parenting Orders made by virtue of an Anti-Social Behaviour Orders, appeals are to the Crown Court [s.10 (1) (b) CDA 1998].

■ In either case the court may:
  • Make such orders as may be necessary to give effect to its determination of the appeal and
  • Also make such incidental or consequential orders as appears to it to be just [s.10(2) CDA 1998]

NB. Any order made by the High Court or Crown Court in response to an appeal (other than one directing an application be re-heard by a magistrates' court) is to be treated as if it were an order of the court from which appeal was brought, not an order of the High Court or Crown Court [s.10(3) CDA 1998].

- A person in respect of whom a Parenting Order is made for failure to secure regular school attendance has the same right of appeal as if the order were a sentence passed on her/him for the offence which led to the order [s.10 (5) CDA 1998].

- A person in respect of whom a Parenting Order is made where a child/young person is convicted of an offence has the same right to appeal as if the offence were an offence committed by her/him and the order were a sentence passed on her/him for the offence [s.10 (4) CDA 1998].

NB. The Lord Chancellor is empowered to make provision in appeals relating to Parenting Orders, made by virtue of Child Safety Orders, about transfer of cases to alternative courts [s.10 (6) CDA 1998].

Child Safety Orders

▨ A court cannot make a Child Safety Order unless previously notified by the Secretary of State that arrangements for implementing them are available and have not been withdrawn [s.11 (2) CDA 1998]. A Home Office letter dated 27.04.00 confirmed arrangements in place in all areas from 01.06.00.

▨ Child Safety Order proceedings are 'family proceedings' for purposes of Children Act 1989 or s.65 Magistrates Courts Act 1980 and standard of proof is as per civil proceedings [s.11 (6) CDA 1998].

Conditions [s.11 (1); (2); (3) CDA 1998]

▨ A magistrates' court, on the application of a local authority may make a Child Safety Order with respect to a child of less than 10 years old if one or more of the following conditions are satisfied:
- S/he has committed an act which if s/he were ten or over would have been an offence
- A Child Safety Order is necessary for the purpose of preventing such an act
- S/he has contravened a ban imposed by a Curfew Notice
- S/he has acted in a manner that caused or was likely to cause harassment, alarm or distress to one or more persons not of her/his own household.

Duration [s.11 (4) CDA 1998]

■ Maximum period is normally 3 months or, where the court is satisfied that the circumstances are exceptional, 12 months.

Effect [s.11 (1); (5) CDA 1998]

■ A Child Safety Order:
- Places the child for a period (not exceeding the permitted maximum) specified in the order, under the supervision of the responsible officer i.e. a local authority social worker or a member of the local YOT and
- Requires the child to comply with such requirements as are specified

■ The requirements that may be specified are those which the court considers desirable in the interests of:
- Securing that the child receives appropriate care, protection and support and is subject to proper control or
- Preventing any repetition of the kind of behaviour which led to the Child Safety Order being made

Procedural Requirements [s.12 CDA 1998]

■ Before making a Child Safety Order, a magistrates' court must obtain and consider information about child's family circumstances and likely effect of the order on those circumstances [s.12 (1) CDA 1998].

■ Before making a Child Safety Order a magistrates' court must explain to the parent/guardian of the child in ordinary language:
  • The effect of the order and the requirements proposed to be included in it
  • The consequences which may follow if the child fails to comply with any of those requirements and
  • That the court has power to review the order on the application of either the parent/guardian or the responsible officer [s.12(2) CDA 1998]

  NB. Requirements included must as far as practicable, avoid any conflict with the parent's religious beliefs and any interference with the times, if any, at which the child attends school [s.12 (3) CDA 1998].

Variation and Discharge [s.12 (4); (5) CDA 1998]

■ If, while the Child Safety Order is in force, it appears to the court which made it, on the application of the responsible officer or parent/guardian, that it is appropriate to do so, the court may make an order to:
  • Discharge the Child Safety Order or
  • Vary it by cancelling any provision included or by inserting (in addition to or in substitution for any of its provisions) any provision that could have been included in the order if the court had then had the power to make it and were exercising that power [s.12(4) CDA 1998]

NB. Where an application to discharge or vary is dismissed, no further application for its discharge can be made under s.12 (4) by any person except with the consent of the court which made the order [s.12(5) CDA 1998].

Failure to Comply with Requirements [s.12 (6) CDA 1998]

■ Where a Child Safety Order is in force and it is proved to the satisfaction of the court which made it (or another magistrates' court acting for same petty sessions area), on the application of the responsible officer, that the child has failed to comply with any requirements included in the order, the court may:
  • Discharge the order and make a Care Order under s.31(1)(a) CA 1989 or
  • Cancel any provision in it or insert in it (in addition to or in substitution for any of its provisions) any provisions that could have been included in the order if the court had then had the power to make it and were exercising the power.

NB. The court may make the s.31(1)(a) CA 1989 Care Order cited above whether or not the conditions contained in s.31(2) of that Act are fulfilled [s.12(7) CDA 1998].

Appeals [s.13 CDA 1998]

■ Appeals must be to the High Court against the making by a magistrates' court of a Child Safety Order, and on such an appeal the High Court:

- May make such orders as may be necessary to give effect to its determination of the appeal and
- May also make such incidental or consequential orders as appear to it to be just [s.13(1) CDA 1998]

NB. Any order of the High Court made on an appeal under s.12 CDA 1998 (other than one directing that an application be re-heard by a magistrates' court), must for purposes of variation, discharge or failure to comply proceedings, be treated as if it were an order of the magistrates' court from which the appeal was brought and not an order of the High Court [s.13 (2) CDA 1998].

Local Child Curfew Schemes [s.14 CDA 1998 as amended by ss.48 & 49 CJPA 2001]

■ A local authority or chief officer of police in accordance with the scheme and any required consultation, may make a 'local child curfew scheme' so as to enable the local authority/officer to give a notice imposing a 'child curfew'.

Effect

■ A ban on children of specified ages under 16 being in a public place in a specified area during specified hours between 9pm and 6am unless under effective control of parent or responsible person 18 or over.

NB. A notice may specify different hours in relation to children of different ages [s.14 (6) CDA 1998].

Duration [s.14 (1) CDA 1998]

■ A specified period not exceeding 90 days.

Procedural Requirements

■ Before making a local child curfew scheme, a local authority must consult:
  • Every chief officer of police any part of whose police area lies within its area and
  • Such other persons/bodies as it considers appropriate

- Before making a local child curfew scheme, a chief officer of police must consult:
    - Every local authority any part of whose area lies within the area to be specified and
    - Such other persons or bodies as s/he considers appropriate

- Notice of curfews must be given:
    - By posting notices in some conspicuous place/s within the specified area
    - In such other manner, if any, as appears to the local authority or chief officer of police to be desirable to provide publicity [s.14(7) CDA 1998]

NB. A scheme will not take effect until submitted to the Secretary of State who may confirm it, or refuse to confirm and may fix a date on which a scheme is to come into operation. If no date is fixed, the scheme will come into operation 1 month after the date of its confirmation.

Contravention [s.15 CDA 1998]

- A constable who has reasonable cause to believe that a child is in contravention of a ban imposed by a Curfew Notice:
    - Must as soon as practicable, inform the local authority for the area that the child has contravened the ban;
    - May remove the child to the child's place of residence unless s/he has reasonable cause to believe that the child would, if removed to that place, be likely to suffer significant harm.

NB. In the latter case, the local authority are obliged to make such enquiries as they consider necessary as soon as practicable and in any case within 48 hours of receiving the information to enable them to decide whether they should take any action to safeguard or promote the child's welfare [s.47 (1) (a)(iii) CA 1989 as inserted by s.15(4) CDA 1998].

Removal of Truants to Designated Premises [s.16 CDA 1998 as amended]

- A constable may remove a child/young person to 'designated premises' or to school from which s/he is absent if the officer has reasonable cause to believe that the individual found by her/him in a public place in a specified area during a specified period is:
  - Of compulsory school age and
  - Absent from school without lawful authority [s.16(3) CDA 1998]

  NB. Absence from school is assumed to be without lawful authority unless justified by leave, sickness, unavoidable cause or a day set apart for religious observation [s.16 (4) CDA 1998].

- A police officer is able to exercise this power when:
  - The local authority has designated a place/s for this purpose and notified the chief officer of police
  - An officer of Superintendent rank or above has specified an area and time period in which this power can be used [s.16(1);(2) CDA 1998]

  NB. S.75 PRA 2002 introduced similar powers for a British Transport Police.

Functions of Courts

■ The CDA 1998 introduced a number of measures designed to reduce delays e.g. bringing cases to court promptly, allowing C.P.S. non-legal staff to undertake certain proceedings, extending powers which may be exercised by a single justice or justices' clerks and by providing for cases which must be tried in the Crown Court to be sent there immediately.

Powers of Youth Court [ss.47 CDA 1998 (as amended by Sch.12 PCCSA 2000; 48; 51 CDA 1998]

■ Where a young person who appears or is brought before a youth court charged with an offence, subsequently attains the age of 18, the court may at any time before start of trial remit her/him for trial to a magistrates' court (other than a youth court) acting for the same petty sessions area as the youth court.

NB. A person thus remitted has no right of appeal against that decision and the other court may deal with the case in any way in which it has power as if all the proceedings had taken place before it.

■ In relation to an indictable-only offence magistrates may send for trial to the Crown Court a juvenile charged jointly with an adult, where they consider that it is in the interests of justice for the juvenile to be tried jointly with that adult [s.51 (5) CDA 1998].

- District Judges (magistrates' courts) sitting in inner London or City of London are able to sit alone in youth courts [Sch.2 CYPA 1933 amended by s.48 CDA 1998]. Equivalent provision exists for District Judges in rest of England and Wales via amendments to Youth Courts (Constitution) Rules 1954.

Sexual or Violent Offenders [ss.59; 60 CDA 1998 & s.85 PCCSA 2000]

- Extended post-release supervision for sexual or violent offenders was introduced by the CDA 1998 and consolidated by PCCSA 2000.

- The court has power to add extended post-release supervision to the sentence it would normally impose on a person convicted of a sexual or violent offence on/after 30.09.98. It may do so where it considers the sentence it would otherwise impose would not provide sufficient time to prevent further offending and secure rehabilitation of offender.

- In such case, the court may pass an 'extended sentence', comprising normal period of imprisonment and supervision ('custodial term') followed by an 'extension period' when offender will continue to be on licence.

  NB. Extension period maximum: Sex offenders = 10 years, violent offenders = 5 years [s.85 PCCSA 2000. An extended sentence must remain within maximum penalty available for offence in question.

Dealing with Offenders

Drug Treatment and Testing Orders (DTTOs) [ss.52–58 PCCSA 2000]

■ The DTTO is a new community order (as defined in s.33 PCCSA 2000) aimed at those convicted of crimes related to their drug habit and who show a willingness to co-operate with treatment.

Conditions for Imposition [s.52 PCCSA 2000]

■ A court may make a DTTO if it is satisfied with respect to a person aged 16 or over, convicted of an offence committed on or after 30.09.98 (other than one fixed by law) that:
- S/he is dependent on or has a propensity to misuse drugs and
- Her/his dependency/propensity is such as requires and may be susceptible to treatment [s.52(1)-(3) PCCSA 2000]

■ A court cannot make a DTTO unless notified by Secretary of State that arrangements for implementing it are available and notice has not been withdrawn [s.52 (5) PCCSA 2000].

NB. Courts were notified by the Home Office on 19.09.00 that such orders were available from 01.10.00.

■ For purposes of ascertaining if the offender has any drug in her/his body, the court may by order require samples of whatever description it may specify, but cannot do so unless offender expresses willingness to comply with its requirements [s.52(4) PCCSA 2000].

Effect & Duration [s.52(1) & 53 PCCSA 2000]

- A DTTO will have effect for a period specified in the order of not less than 6 months and no more than 3 years (the 'treatment and testing period') and may include requirements and provisions detailed below.

- 'Treatment requirement' is that the offender must submit, during all of the 'treatment and testing period' to treatment by/under direction of a specified and suitably qualified/experienced 'treatment provider' with a view to reduction/elimination of dependency/propensity to misuse drugs [s.53(1) PCCSA 2000].

- 'Required treatment' for any particular period must specify whether residential, but the nature of it is not otherwise be specified [s.53 (2) PCCSA 2000].

- For the purposes of ascertaining if s/he has any drug in her/his body during the treatment and testing period, the testing requirement means offender is obliged to provide such samples at such times or in such circumstances as may (subject to provisions of the order) be determined by the 'treatment provider' [s.53(4) PCCSA 2000].

- A DTTO will specify the minimum number of tests per month [s.53 (5) PCCSA 2000].

- A DTTO will:
  - Provide for its duration, that the offender will be supervised by a probation officer for/assigned to the petty sessions area specified in the order;
  - Require the offender to keep in touch with the probation officer in accordance with such instructions as may be given to notify her/him of any change of address;
  - Provide that the results of the tests carried out on the samples of provided by the offender in pursuance of the testing requirement will be communicated to the probation officer [s.54 (1) PCCSA 2000].

- Supervision by the responsible officer is to be carried out only to such an extent as may be necessary to enable her/him to:
  - Report to the court responsible for the order, on the offender's progress and on any failure by the offender to comply with requirements of the order
  - Determine whether the circumstances are such that s/he should apply to that court for the revocation/amendment of the order [s.54 (5) PCCSA 2000].

- A court intending to make a DTTO must explain to the offender in ordinary language:
  - The effect of the order and of the requirements proposed to be included in it;
  - The consequences if s/he fails to comply with any of those requirements;

- That the order may be reviewed on the application of the offender or the responsible officer and that
- The order will be periodically reviewed at intervals as provided for in the order or by virtue of s.54(6) PCCSA 2000 [s.52(6) PCCSA 2000]
- And that the court will not make the order unless the offender expresses willingness to comply with its requirements [s.52 (7) PCCSA 2000].

Periodic Review [s.54 (6) PCCSA 2000]

- At intervals of not less than monthly a DTTO must be reviewed, usually at a 'review hearing' held for this purpose by the court responsible for the Order.

- The offender is required to attend each review hearing where the court will consider a written report about her/his progress (including test results and views provided by the treatment provider) from the responsible officer.

NB. If at a review hearing, the court having heard the responsible officer's report is of the opinion the offender's progress is satisfactory, it may amend the order to provide for each subsequent review to be made by the court without a hearing [s.55(6) PCCSA 2000]. Similarly, if unhappy with the offender's progress the court may re-instate hearings [s.55 (7) PCCSA 2000].

- At a review hearing, the court having considered the responsible officer's report:
  - May amend any requirement/provision of order
  - Cannot amend treatment or testing requirement unless offender expresses a willingness to comply
  - Cannot amend any provision of order so as to exceed the treatment and testing minimum and maximum periods
  - Must not, except with consent of offender amend any requirements or provisions of order while an appeal against it is pending [s.55(1)-(2) PCCSA 2000]

- If the offender fails to express willingness to comply with the treatment/testing requirements as proposed to be amended by the court, it may:
  - Revoke the order
  - Deal with offender for offence in respect of which order was made in any manner in which it could have dealt with her/him if s/he had just been convicted by the court of the offence [s52(3) PCCSA 2000].

NB. In dealing with the offender in the way described immediately above, the court must take into account the extent to which the offender has complied with the requirements of the order and may impose a custodial sentence regardless of the constraints of the provisions of s.79(2) PCCSA 2000 [s.55(4) PCCSA 2000].

Reprimands and Warnings [ss.65; 66 CDA 1998]

- 'Reprimands' and 'warnings' replaced formal 'cautioning' of young offenders.

Criteria for Issuing [s.65 (1) CDA 1998]

- Before a police officer can issue a reprimand or a warning, the following 5 criteria must be satisfied:
  - Police have evidence that a child/young person (the offender) has committed an offence
  - Police consider the evidence to be such that there would be a realistic chance of prosecution
  - Offender admits to police s/he has committed the offence
  - Offender has not previously been convicted of an offence and
  - Police are satisfied that it would not be in the public interest for the offender to be prosecuted.

- Where the offender has not previously been reprimanded or warned police may **reprimand** her/him.

- The police may **warn** the offender if:
  - S/he has not previously been warned or
  - The offence was committed more than 2 years after the date of previous warning and they do not consider the offence serious enough to require a charge to be brought but, in these circumstances, nobody may be warned more than once [s.65(3) CDA 1998]

■ Where the offender has not been previously
reprimanded but police consider the offence serious
enough, they must warn rather than reprimand
her/him [s.65 (4) CDA 1998].

Reprimands/Warnings

No previous reprimand or warning police may reprimand

No previous warning or offence   police may warn
more than 2 years after date of
previous warning

No previous reprimand but police   police must warn
consider offence serious enough   rather than
to require a warning   reprimand

■ The police are obliged:
  • To give any reprimand or warning at a police
    station
  • Where the offender is under 17, to administer it
    in the presence of an appropriate adult
  • To explain to the offender (and where relevant
    the appropriate adult) in ordinary language the
    effects of reprimands and warnings respectively
    on any future offences within 2 years as per s.66
    which is explained below [s.65(5) CDA 1998]

*NB. For the above purposes, an appropriate adult
means a parent/guardian; if in the care of a local
authority or voluntary organisation a representative
of that organisation; a social worker of a local
authority social services department, or, if none of*

these is available, any responsible person aged 18 or over who is not a police officer or employed by the police.[s.65(7) CDA 1998].

■ The Secretary of State is obliged to publish guidance on give reprimands or warnings e.g. seriousness of offence, rank of police officer to administer them, the form they should take etc.[s.65(6) CDA 1998](see 'Final Warning Scheme: Guidance for Police and YOTS' published jointly by Home Office and YJB November 2002).

NB. Important issues of principle about reprimands/ warnings were raised in R (U) v Metropolitan Police Commissioner. Juveniles, having admitted offences of indecent assault, received a 'final warning' without their explicit consent and without being informed that their response would require their registration under the Sex Offenders' Act 1997.

In a judicial review of the above case, the Court considered that the Secretary of State's guidance was flawed. The Court stated that the appropriate practice is to ensure that before a reprimand or final warning is administered, the offender and parent, carer or other appropriate adult should be told of the consequences and asked whether or not they consent to that course of action.

Effects [s.66 CDA 1998]

■ When police warn an offender they must, as soon as practicable refer her/him to a YOT [s.66 (1) CDA 1998].

▪ A YOT must assess any such person and unless they consider it inappropriate to do so, must arrange for her/him to participate in a rehabilitation programme [s.66 (2) CDA 1998].

NB. The Secretary of State must issue guidance about what is to be included in such rehabilitation programmes, the manner in which any failure by a person to participate in such a programme is to be recorded and the person to who any such failure is to be notified [s.66(3) CDA 1998].

▪ Where a person who has received a warning under s.65 is convicted of an offence committed within 2 years of the warning, the court:
  • Cannot grant a conditional discharge for the offence unless it is of the opinion that there are exceptional circumstances relating to the offence/offender which justify it (and where it does so, must state in open court it is of that opinion and why) [s.66(4) CDA 1998 as amended by Sch.9 para. 198 PCCSA 2000]

NB. Any reprimand, warning or failure to participate in a rehabilitation programme arrange for her/him under s.65 may be cited in criminal proceedings in the same circumstances as conviction of the person may be cited [s.66(5) CDA 1998].

Non-Custodial Orders

Reparation Orders [ss.73–75 PCCSA 2000]

- The court cannot make a Reparation Order unless notified by Secretary of State that arrangements for implementing such orders are available and notice has not been withdrawn [s.73(6) PCCSA 2000]. All courts were notified in a Home Office letter dated 27.04.00 that such orders were available from 01.06.00.

- Where a child/young person is convicted of an offence other than one for which the sentence is fixed by law, the court may, subject to conditions described below impose a Reparation Order requiring the offender to make reparation specified in the order to:
  - Person/s specified or
  - Community at large [s.73(1);(2) PCCSA 2000]

  NB. The court cannot make a Reparation Order if it proposes to pass a custodial sentence or make a Community Punishment Order, Community Punishment and Rehabilitation Order, Supervision Order which includes requirements under Sch.6 PCCSA 2000 or an Action Plan or Referral Order [s.73(4) PCCSA 2000].

Procedural Requirements

- Before making a Reparation Order, a court must obtain and consider a written report from a probation officer, social worker of a local authority social services or a member of a YOT indicating:
  - Type of work which is suitable for the offender
  - Attitude of victim/s to the requirements proposed to be included in the order [s.73(5) PCCSA 2000]

- Before making a Reparation Order, a court must explain to the offender in ordinary language:
  - The effect of the order and of the requirements proposed to be included in it
  - The consequences of failure to comply (detailed in Sch.8 of the PCCSA 2000)
  - That the court has the power to review the order on the application of the offender or of the responsible officer [s.73(7) PCCSA 2000]

Effect/ Duration [s. 74 PCCSA 2000]

- Requirements specified in a Reparation Order must, so far as is practicable be such as to avoid any:
  - Conflict with the offender's religious beliefs or with the requirements of any Community Order to which s/he may be subject
  - Interference with the times of school/work/college attendance [s.74(3) PCCSA 2000]

- A Reparation Order cannot require the offender to work for more than 24 hours in aggregate or to make reparation to any person without the consent of that person [s.74 (1) PCCSA 2000].

- Any requirements specified must in the opinion of the court be commensurate with seriousness of the offence or combination of offence and one or more offences associated with it [s.74 (2) PCCSA 2000].

- Any reparation required by a Reparation Order must be supervised by a responsible officer (probation officer, social worker of a local authority social services or member of a YOT) and be made within 3 months of order being made [s.74(8) PCCSA 2000].

  NB. The court must give reasons if it does not make a Reparation Order in a case where it has the power to do so [s.73 (8) PCCSA 2000].

Failure to Comply with Requirements [Sch.8 PCCSA 2000]

- If the appropriate court (the youth court for the area where the offender resides/will reside) is satisfied, on the application of the responsible officer that the offender has failed to comply with any requirement included in the order it may:
  - (Whether or not it varies or revokes the order) fine the offender or make an Attendance Centre Order or Curfew Order
  - If the Reparation Order was made by a youth court, revoke it and deal with her/him for

original offence in any manner in which s/he could have been dealt with for that offence by the first court

- If the Reparation Order was made by the Crown Court, commit her/him to custody or release on bail until s/he can appear before the Crown Court [Sch.8 para.2 PCCSA 2000]

NB. In dealing with a failure to comply with an order, a court must take into account the extent to which the offender has complied with its requirements [Sch.8 para.2 (7) PCCSA 2000].

- If it appears to the appropriate court (the youth court for the area in which the offender resides/will reside), on application of the responsible officer or offender that it is appropriate to do, it may revoke or vary the Reparation Order by:
  - Cancelling any provision in it or
  - Inserting in it (in addition to or in substitution for any provisions) any provision it could have included if the court had then had power to make it and had exercised that power [Sch.8 para.5(1) PCCSA 2000]

NB. If an application to revoke is dismissed, no further application for its discharge can be made by any person except with the consent of the appropriate court [Sch.8 para.5 (3) PCCSA 2000].

Action Plan Orders [ss.69–72 PCCSA 2000]

■ The court cannot make an Action Plan Order unless notified by Secretary of State that arrangements for such orders are available and notice has not been withdrawn [s.69.(7) PCCSA 2000].

NB. All courts were notified in a Home Office letter dated 27.04.00 that such orders were available from 01.06.00.

■ Where a child/young person is convicted of an offence, the court may (subject to conditions described below), if it is of the opinion that it is desirable to do so in the interests of securing her/his rehabilitation or preventing further offences, make an Action Plan Order.

NB. The court must not make an Action Plan Order if the offender is already subject of such an order or the court proposed to pass on her/him a custodial or make a Community Rehabilitation Order, Community Punishment Order, Community Punishment and Rehabilitation Order, an Attendance Centre Order a Supervision Order, or a Referral Order or [s.69(5) PCCSA 2000].

Procedural Requirements

■ Before making an Action Plan Order a court must obtain and consider a written report by a probation officer, social worker from a local authority social services department or a member of a YOT indicating:

- The requirements proposed by that person to be included in the order
- The benefits to the offender that the proposed requirements are designed to achieve and
- The attitude of parent/guardian of the offender to the proposed requirements and
- Where the offender is under 16, information about the offender's family circumstances and the likely effect of the order on these circumstances [s.69(6) PCCSA 2000]

▨ Before making an Action Plan Order, a court must explain to the offender in ordinary language:

- The effect of the order and of the requirements proposed to be included in it
- The consequences which may follow (under Sch.8) if s/he fails to comply with any of those requirements
- That the court has power under Sch.8 to review the order on the application either of the offender or responsible officer [s.69(11) PCCSA 2000]

Effect/ Duration

▨ The Action Plan Order:

- Requires the offender for a period of 3 months beginning with the date of the order to comply with an 'action plan' i.e. a series of requirements with respect to her/his actions and whereabouts in that period

- Places the offender under the supervision for that period of the responsible officer and
- Requires the offender to comply with any directions given to her/him by that officer with a view to implementation of that plan [s.69(1) PCCSA 2000]

- Requirements included in an Action Plan Order or directions given by a responsible officer may require the offender to do all or any of the following:
  - To participate in specified activities
  - To present her/himself at specified place/s and/or time/s
  - (Where the offence is punishable with imprisonment in the case of those age 21 or over) to attend an Attendance Centre for specified hours
  - To stay away from specified place/s
  - To comply with any specified arrangements for her/his education
  - To make specified reparations to specified person/s or to the community at large
  - To attend any hearing fixed by the court under s.71 PCCSA 2000 (designed to review the effectiveness of the order) [s.70(1) PCCSA 2000]

NB. With respect to a young person aged 14 or over who agrees to it, the court will be [not yet in force] empowered to impose drug treatment/testing requirements [s.70(4A)-(4H) PCCSA 2000 introduced by Sch.24 CJA 2003].

▣ The above requirements and directions must as far as is practicable, avoid any conflict with offender's religious beliefs or with requirements of any other Community Orders to which s/he may be subject and any interference with times (if any) of normal school/work/college attendance [s.70(5) PCCSA 2000].

▣ A person may not be specified as the recipient of reparation in requirements or directions unless:
  • S/he is identified by the court or responsible officer as the victim of the offence or a person otherwise affected by it
  • S/he consents to the reparation being made [s.70(4) PCCSA 2000]

Review [s.71 (1) PCCSA 2000]

▣ Immediately after making an Action Plan Order a court may:
  • Fix a further hearing date not more than 21 days after the making of the order and
  • Direct the responsible officer to present a report as to the effectiveness of the order and the extent to which it has been implemented.

▣ At such a review hearing, the court:
  • Must consider the responsible officer's report
  • May on the application of the responsible officer or offender, vary the order by cancelling any provision in it or by inserting in it (in addition to or in substitution for any of its provisions) any provision that the court could originally have included in it [s.71(2) PCCSA 2000]

Failure to Comply with Requirements & Variation & Discharge [Sch.8 PCCSA 2000]

■ If the appropriate court (the youth court for the area where the offender resides/will reside) is satisfied, on the application of the responsible officer that the offender has failed to comply with any requirement included in the order it may:

- (Whether or not it varies or revokes the order) fine the offender a maximum of £1000 or make an Attendance Centre Order or Curfew Order;
- If the Action Plan Order was made by a youth court, revoke the order and deal with her/him for the original offence in any manner in which s/he could have been dealt with for that offence by the first court
- If the Action Plan Order was made by the Crown Court, commit her/him to custody or release on bail until s/he can appear before the Crown Court [Sch.8 para.2 PCCSA 2000].

NB. In dealing with a failure to comply with an order, a court must take into account the extent to which offender has complied with its requirements [Sch.8 para.2 (7) PCCSA 2000].

■ If it appears to the appropriate court (the youth court for the area in which the offender resides/will reside), on the application of the responsible officer or the offender that it is appropriate to do, it may revoke or vary the Action Plan Order by:
Cancelling any provision in it or
Inserting in it (in addition to or in substitution for

any of its provisions) any provision that it could have included in the order if the court had then had power to make it and had exercised that power [Sch.8 para.5(1) PCCSA 2000]

NB. Where an application to revoke an Action Plan Order is dismissed, no further application for its revocation can be made by any person except with the consent of the appropriate court [Sch.8 para.5(3) PCCSA 2000].

Curfew Orders [ss.37–40 PCCSA 2000]

■ Where a person is convicted, the court may (subject to restrictions in ss.34–36 PCCSA 2000) make an order requiring her/him to remain for periods specified at a specified place [s.37(1) PCCSA 2000].

■ A Curfew Order may specify different places or different periods for different days but must not specify periods:
  • Beyond 6 months of order being made or
  • Which amount to less than 2 or more than 12 hours in any day [s.37(3) PCCSA 2000]

NB. Requirements shall as far as practicable avoid any conflict with offender's religious beliefs, requirements of any other Community Order to which s/he may be subject and any interference with times, if any at which s/he normally works or attends school [s.37(5) PCCSA 2000].

■ A court cannot make a Curfew Order unless notified

by Secretary of State arrangements for monitoring offenders' whereabouts are available and notification has not been withdrawn [s.37(7) PCCSA 2000] (all forms of curfew became available throughout England and Wales by 01.12.01).

- Before making a Curfew Order the court must obtain and consider information about the place proposed to be specified (including information as to attitude of persons likely to be affected by the enforced presence of the offender there) [s.37(8) PCCSA 2000].

- Before making a Curfew Order in respect of an offender aged under 16, the court must obtain and consider information about her/his family circumstances and the likely affect of such an order on these circumstances [s.37(9) PCCSA 2000].

- Before making a Curfew Order the court must explain to the offender in ordinary language:
  - The effect of the order (including any additional requirements such as electronic monitoring)
  - The consequences which may follow under Part II of Sch.3 to the PCCSA 2000 if s/he fails to comply with any requirements of the Order and
  - That court has power under Parts III and IV of Sch.3 to review order on application of offender or responsible officer [s.37(10) PCCSA 2000]

NB. Where a court has been notified necessary arrangements had been made in relevant area it is able to include requirements for securing electronic monitoring of offender's whereabouts during the curfew periods specified [s.36B(1) PCCSA 2000 introduced by s.52 CJCSA 2000].

Failure to Comply & Revocation and Amendment [s.39 & Sch.3 PCCSA 2000]

■ If at any time while a Curfew Order is in force in respect of an offender it appears on information to a JP acting for the petty sessions area concerned that the offender has failed to comply with any of the order's requirements, s/he may issue a summons, or if the information is in writing on oath, issue a warrant for the offender's arrest [Sch.3 para.3(1) PCCSA 2000].

■ If proved to the satisfaction of a magistrates' court before which an offender appears/is brought that s/he has failed without reasonable cause to comply with any requirements of the relevant order, the court may:
   • Impose a fine of up to £1,000
   • Where the offender is 16 or over (subject to para.7) make a Community Punishment Order in respect of her/him
   • Where the offender is less than 16 it may (subject to para.8) make an Attendance Centre Order
   • Where the relevant order was made by a magistrates' court, it may deal with her/him for the offence in respect of which the order was made in any way it could have dealt with her/him if s/he had just been convicted by the court of the offence [Sch.3 para.4 PCCSA 2000]

Supervision Orders [s.63 & Sch.6 PCCSA 2000]

Criteria

■ Where a child/young person is convicted of an offence and the court is satisfied that s/he resides/will reside in the area of the local authority, it may place her/him under the supervision of:
- The local authority designated by the order
- A probation officer;
- A member of the YOT

■ The above officer must advice, assist and befriend the offender [ss.63 (1); 64(4) PCCSA 2000].

NB. The court must not designate a local authority as supervisor unless that local authority agrees or it appears that the offender does or will reside in that authority's area. [s.64 (1) PCCSA 2000].

Duration

■ A Supervision Order, unless revoked or specified for a shorter period will last 3 years from the date it is made [s.63 (7) PCCSA 2000].

NB. Nothing in the PCCSA 2000 prevents a court which makes a Supervision Order also making a Curfew Order with respect to the offender [s.64A introduced by Sch.2 para. 3 ASBA 2003].

Requirements to Comply With Directions of Supervisor/ Live With A Named Individual

■ A Supervision Order may (assuming that the court is satisfied there is a local authority scheme as per s.66 PCCSA 2000) require the offender to comply with directions of the supervisor requiring any or all of the following, to:
  - Live at place/s specified for specified period/s of time
  - Present her/himself to person/s specified in the directions at place/s and on day/s specified
  - Participate in specified activities on specified days [Sch.6 para.2(2) PCCSA 2000]

■ With respect to a young person of 14 or over who consents, a court is empowered to impose drug treatment/testing requirements [Sch.6 para. 6A PCCSA 2000 introduced by Sch.24 CJA 2003]

■ The total number of days in respect of which an offender may be required to comply with such directions must not exceed 180, or fewer if so specified in the Supervision Order [Sch.6 para.2(5) PCCSA 2000 as amended by Sch.2 para.4 ASBA 2003].

  NB. Any day on which directions given were not complied with does not count toward the total allowable [Sch.3 para. 2(6) PCCSA 2000].

■ A Supervision Order may also require an offender to reside with a named individual (who agrees to the requirement) so long as this is consistent with other more general requirements of the supervising officer [Sch.6 para.1 PCCSA 2000].

Requirements as to Activities, Reparation

■ Unless the Supervision Order requires the offender to comply with directions given by the supervisor under Sch.6 para.2(1) PCCSA 2000 (see above), it may for a maximum of 180 days require the offender to:
  · Live at specified place/s for specified period/s
  · Present her/himself to specified person/s at specified place/s on specified day/s
  · Participate in specified activities on day/s so specified
  · Make reparation specified in the order to person/s specified and/or to the community at large
  · Refrain from participating in activities specified in the order on specified day/s or for a portion or all of the period of the Supervision Order [Sch.6 para.3 PCCSA 2000 as amended by Sch.2 para.3 ASBA 2003]

NB. Reparation = reparation for the offence other than by payment of compensation.

Requirements to Live For Specified Period in Local Authority Accommodation [Sch.6 para.5 PCCSA 2000]

■ Where the following conditions are satisfied, a Supervision Order may impose for a maximum of 6 months a 'Local Authority Residence Requirement' which compels the offender to live for a specified period in local authority accommodation:

- A Supervision Order has previously been made with respect to the offender
- That Supervision Order imposed requirements (other than one for treatment for a mental condition) or a 'Local Authority Requirement' with which the offender has failed to comply or
- The offender was convicted of an offence whilst that order was in force and
- The court is satisfied that the failure to comply or the behaviour which constituted the offence was due to a significant extent to the circumstances in which the offender was living (not applicable if the offender already in local authority accommodation) and
- That imposition of a Local Authority Residence Requirement will assist in her/his rehabilitation.

NB. The court must consult the designated local authority before imposing the residence requirement [Sch.6 para.5 (4) PCCSA 2000].

▦ Further potential requirements for treatment for mental conditions and for education are provided for in Sch.6 paras.6–7 PCCSA 2000.

Requirement to Live for a Specified Period in with Local Authority Foster Parent [Sch.6 para. 5A PCCSA 2000 inserted by Sch.2 para.4 ASBA 2003]

▦ A Supervision order may impose a 'Foster Parent

Residence Requirement 'that the offender must live for a specified period with a local authority foster parent, if:

* The offence is punishable with imprisonment in the case of an offender aged 18 or over
* The offence, or combination of it and one or more associated offences, was so serious that a custodial sentence would normally be appropriate (or in the case of a 10 or 11 year old child, would be so if the offender were 12 or over) **and**
* The court is satisfied that the behaviour which constituted the offence was due to a significant extent to the circumstances in which the offender was living and that imposition of the requirement will assist rehabilitation

▪ A Foster Parent Residence Requirement must designate the local authority which is to place the offender under s.23 (2) (a) CA 1989 which will be the authority in which the offender resides.

▪ A court cannot impose a residence requirement unless notified by the Secretary of state that arrangements are in place and unless it has consulted the designated local authority.

NB. Unless extended as a result of a breach, the maximum period is 12 months.

Breach/ Revocation & Amendment [Sch.7 para.2 PCCSA 2000 as amended]

- If the court is satisfied on the application of the supervisor that an offender has failed to comply with any requirements it may (whether or not it revokes or amends the Supervision Order):
  - Fine the offender up to £1,000
  - Impose a Curfew Order (unless offender is already subject to a Curfew Order)
  - Impose an Attendance Centre Order
  - If the Supervision Order was made by a magistrates' court, revoke it and deal with the offence in any way which had been available when the order was made
  - If the Supervision Order was made by the Crown court, commit the offender in custody or release on bail until s/he can be brought or appear before the Crown Court.

- In relation to a Supervision Order imposing a Foster Parent Residence Requirement, the court may extend the period specified in the requirement to a period of not more than 18 months beginning on which the requirement first took effect [Sch.7 para.5(2A) PCCSA 2000 inserted by Sch.2 para. 4 ASBA 2003]

  NB. The court must take into account the extent to which the offender has complied with the requirements of the Supervision Order [Sch.7 para.2 (7) PCCSA 2000].

- On the application of supervisor or offender (or

parent on behalf of a child/young person), the court may revoke or amend the Supervision Order by cancelling any requirement in it or inserting any provision which could have been included [Sch.7 para.5 PCCSA 2000].

NB. Sch.7 PCCSA 2000 contains further restrictions on the court's powers to revoke/amend Supervision Orders.

Referral Orders [Part III PCCSA 2000]

Definition of Referral Order

■ A 'Referral Order' is a compulsory or discretionary referral made under s.16(2) or (3) PCCSA 2000, by the court to a youth offender panel in circumstances where:
- Neither the offence or any connected offence is one for which the sentence is fixed by law
- The court is not proposing to impose a custodial sentence or make a Hospital Order and
- The court is not proposing to discharge the child/young person absolutely

NB. Referral is available to a court only if it has been notified by the Secretary of State that arrangements for implementation of such Orders are available in the area in which it appears to the court that the offender does or will live, and that the notification has not been withdrawn [s.17(5) PCCSA 2000].

Compulsory Referral Conditions [s.17 (1) PCCSA 2000 as amended]

■ A Referral Order is compulsory if the offence is an imprisonable one and the offender;
- Pleaded guilty to the offence and to any connected offence
- Has never been convicted by or before a court in the UK of any offence other than the offence and any connected offence and
- Has never been bound over in criminal proceedings in England and Wales or Northern Ireland to keep the peace or be of good behaviour

Discretionary Referral Conditions [s.17 (2) PCCSA 2000]

■ A Referral Order is discretionary if:
- The offence is a non-imprisonable one and the conditions for a compulsory referral in the case of an imprisonable offence are satisfied, or
- The offender is being dealt with by the court for the offence (imprisonable or not) and one or more connected offences
- Although s/he has pleaded guilty to at least one of the offences, s/he has pleaded not guilty to at least one of them
- S/he has never been convicted by a court in the UK of any offence other than the offence and/or any connected offence and
- S/he has never been bound over in criminal

proceedings in England and Wales or Northern Ireland to keep the peace or be of good behaviour

NB. The Secretary of State is empowered to issue regulations to refine further the description of relevant offenders e.g. by age, plea, offence/s, previous convictions, previous disposals, other characteristics, behaviours of or circumstances relating to any person who has at any time been charged in the same proceedings as the offender [s.17(3);(4) PCCSA 2000].

NB. The Referral Orders (Amendments of Referral Conditions) Regulations 2003 S1 2003/1605 have been issued and are reflected in the conditions set out above.

Procedures [s.18 PCCSA 2000]

- A Referral Order must:
  - Specify the YOT responsible for implementing the order
  - Require the offender to attend each of the meetings of the youth offender panel to be established by the team for the offender and
  - Specify the period for which any youth offender contract is to last (minimum 3, maximum 12 months) [s.18(1) PCCSA 2000]

- On making a Referral Order the court must explain in ordinary language:
  - The effect of the order and

- The consequences if no youth offender contract takes effect between offender and panel or if the offender breaches any of the terms of any such contract [s.18(3) PCCSA 2000]

NB. Although not a statutory requirement, the length of youth offender contracts will in practice be set by the court on the basis of seriousness of offence to ensure that sentence is proportionate to it.

- Where referral is being ordered for 2 or more offences, the court will make a Referral Order for each one, though each order will be supervised by the same youth offender panel and there can only be one youth offender contract [s.18(5) PCCSA 2000].

- Although the period specified in each order may be of a different length, the total time for which any youth offender contract has effect will not exceed 12 months [s.18(6) PCCSA 2000].

- The Referral Order constitutes the entire sentencing for the offence and any associated offences and is not to be treated as an additional sentence to run alongside others although the referral may be accompanied by ancillary orders such as costs, compensation, forfeiting items, exclusions from football matches etc [s.19(2)&(3) PCCSA 2000].

NB. The Referral Order may not be accompanied by a Bind Over for a parent.

Youth Offender Panels [s.21 PCCSA 2000]

■ Where a Referral Order has been made in respect of an offender (or 2 or more associated Referral Orders have been so made), it is the duty of the YOT specified in the orders/s to:
- Establish a youth offender panel for the offender
- Arrange for the first meeting of the panel to be held to agree a contract and subsequently
- To arrange for holding of any further meetings required to review progress or determine a referral back to court is needed [s.21(1) PCCSA 2000]

NB. The Secretary of State will issue guidance on constitution, conduct of proceedings and discharge of functions of panels [s.21 (2) PCCSA 2000].

■ If a parent/guardian of an offender fails to comply with a s.20 'requirement to attend the panel' and the offender is under 18 at the tome of the failure, the panel may refer the parent/guardian to a youth court [s.22(2A) PCCSA 2000 inserted by Sch.34 CJA 2003].

■ The terms of the contract committing an offender to a programme of behaviour may in particular include any of the following:
- Financial or other reparation (subject to their consent) to any person who appears to the panel to be the victim/otherwise affected by the offence/s for which the offender was referred

- • The offender attending mediation sessions with any such victim or other person
- • Carrying out unpaid work or service in or for the community
- • The offender to be at home at a time specified under the programme
- • Attendance at school/college/work;
- • Participation in specified activities e.g. those designed to address offending behaviour or offering education/training or assisting with rehabilitation of those dependent on or misusing alcohol/drugs
- • The offender presenting her/himself to specified persons at times and places specified in or determined by the programme;
- • Staying away from specified place/s and/or person/s
- • Enabling the offender's compliance to be supervised and recorded [s.23(2) PCCSA 2000]

▦ The panel may refer the case back to court if it does not reach agreement as to an appropriate contract at the first or a re-convened meeting, forms the view that there is no realistic chance of so doing or the offender unreasonably refuses to sign a contract which has been agreed [s.25 PCCSA 2000].

▦ Progress meetings may be held to monitor an offender's conduct and any significant change of her/his circumstances and the panel is empowered to refer the offender back to court in the event of an unreasonable failure to co-operate [s.26 PCCSA 2000].

NB. The programme may not provide for the electronic monitoring of the offender's whereabouts or for the offender to have any physical restrictions placed on her/his movements [s.23(3) PCCSA 2000].

Custody: Detention & Training Order

Criteria for Use [s.100 (1) PCCSA 2000]

- The CDA 1998 replaced 'Secure Training Orders' and 'Detention in Young Offender Institutions' with a single custodial sentence for under 18 year olds.

- The court may pass a Detention and Training Order on an offender aged 15 to 17 inc. convicted of an offence punishable in the case of an adult aged 21 or over with imprisonment if:
  - The court is of the opinion that the offence or a combination of the offence and one or more associated with it was so serious that only such a sentence can be justified or
  - In the case of a violent or sexual offence, only such a sentence would be adequate to protect the public from serious harm from the offender [s.79(2) PCCSA 2000] or if
  - The offender refuses to express willingness to comply with conditions of a Community Rehabilitation or Supervision Order or a requirement of a Drug Treatment and Testing Order [s.79(3) PCCSA 2000]

- In the case of a 12 to 14 year old, the court must additionally be satisfied that at the time of the conviction the child/young person is a persistent offender [s.100 (2)(a) PCCSA 2000].

NB. A court may only make a Detention and Training Order for a 10 or 11 year old if of the opinion that only a custodial sentence would be adequate to protect the public from further offending by her/him and the Secretary of State has announced the introduction of this power [s.100(2)(b) PCCSA 2000]. At the time of publication (May 2004) no such announcement has been made.

▪ When making a Detention and Training Order with respect to an under 15 year old, the court must in addition to its duty under s.79(4) PCCSA 2000 state in open court that the relevant criteria of s.100(2) PCCSA 2000 have been met [s.100(4) PCCSA 2000].

Effect & Duration

▪ A Detention and Training Order is an order that the offender will be subject for the term specified to a period of detention and training followed by a period of supervision [s.100(3) PCCSA 2000].

▪ Provided that they do not exceed the maximum that the Crown Court could (in the case of an offender aged 21 or over) impose, both Crown Courts and Magistrates' Courts may impose Orders of 4, 6, 8, 10, 12, 18 or 24 months [s.101(1);(2) PCCSA 2000].

NB. Where the offence is a summary one and the maximum imprisonment a court could (if offender 18 or over) impose is 51 weeks, the term of detention may not exceed 6 months [s101(2A) PCCSA 200 introduced by s.298 CJA 2003] [not yet in force]

■ Concurrent and consecutive Detention and Training Orders can be imposed as if they were sentences of imprisonment but if the term consequently exceeds 24 months, the excess must be treated as remitted [s.101 (3)-(5) PCCSA 2000].

■ In determining the term of detention and training for an offence, the court must take account of any period for which the offender has been remanded in custody in connection with the offence or any other offence the charge for which was founded on the same facts/evidence [s.101(8) PCCSA 2000]

NB. The effect of 'taking account' rather than automatic deduction of remand time will be to ensure that the court can impose sufficient time in custody after sentence to enable engagement with the offender.

■ Custody in this section = held in police detention, remanded or committed to custody by an order of a court, or to local authority accommodation under s.23 CYPA 1969 and kept in secure accommodation, detained in secure training centre pursuant to arrangements under subsection s.23(7A) of that Act, or remanded, admitted or removed to hospital under ss.35, 36, 38 or 48 MHA 1983 [s.101(11) PCCSA 2000 as amended by s.133 CJPA 2001].

NB. A person is in police detention referred to above at any time s/he is detained for purpose of PACE 1984 or under s.14 Prevention of Terrorism (Temporary Provisions) Act 1989.

Periods of Detention, Training & Supervision [ss.102; 103 PCCSA 2000]

▪ An offender must serve the period of detention and training in such secure accommodation as may be determined by the Secretary of State or by another person authorised for this purpose [s.102(1) PCCSA 2000].

▪ Unless varied for the reasons described below, the period of detention and training is half of the term of the order [s.101 (2) PCCSA 2000].

NB. The Secretary of State may release an offender if s/he is satisfied that exceptional circumstances justify this on compassionate grounds [s.101 (3) PCCSA 2000].

▪ The Secretary of State is empowered to release an offender who has been made subject of a Detention and Training Order of:
  - 8 months or more but less than 18 months duration, 1 month before the half-way point of the term of the order; and
  - 18 months or more duration, 1 month or 2 months before the half-way point of the term of the order [s.101(4) PCCSA 2000]

NB. The Secretary of State can also apply to the youth court for late release for periods of the same lengths [s.102 (5) PCCSA 2000].

▪ The period of supervision for an offender subject to a Detention and Training Order begins from the offender's release (whether at the half-way point of the order or otherwise) and, unless the Secretary of State orders that the period is to change for all offenders as per s.103 (2) PCCSA 2000, will end when the order ends [s.103 (1) PCCSA 2000].

▦ Supervision will be undertaken by a social worker of a local authority social services department, a probation officer or a member of a YOT who is to be appointed at the start of the sentence and whose appointment must be notified to the offender together with any requirements with which the offender must comply [s.103 (4)–(7) PCCSA 2000].

Breaches of Supervision Requirements [s.104 PCCSA 2000]

▦ Where a Detention and Training Order is in force in respect of an offender and it appears to a JP acting for a relevant petty sessions area that s/he has failed to comply with requirements under s.103(6)(b) PCCSA 2000, the Justice:
  • May issue a summons requiring the offender to appear at the youth court or
  • If the information is in writing and on oath, may issue a warrant for the offender's arrest requiring her/him to be brought before the youth court

▦ If the court is satisfied that the offender has failed to comply with requirements under s.103(6)(b) PCCSA 2000 it may:
  • Order the offender to be detained for a further period of up to 3 months or until the end of the

Detention and Training Order (whichever is the shorter) or

- Impose a fine of up to level 3 on the standard scale [s.104 (3) PCCSA 2000].

Offences during Currency of Order [s.105 PCCSA 2000]

- If an offender after her/his release but before the order ends commits an offence punishable with imprisonment in the case of a person aged 21 or over(whether or not conviction occurs within the period of the order), the court:
  May impose an additional period of detention
  NB. Maximum length for this detention period is equivalent to the time between date of offence and end of the order. It will be disregarded in sentencing the offender for the new offence but can be served before or concurrently with any new sentence.

Interaction with Sentences of Detention [s.106 PCCA 2000]

- The provisions of s.106 (1)–(5) provide for the position where an offender under 18 years old is subject to 'Detention in a Young Offender Institution' under the former arrangements and who subsequently receives a Detention and Training Order (DTO) as well as for an offender already subject to a DTO who, on attaining 18 years of age receives a sentence of Detention in a Young Offender Institution.

■ If, arising from a court's power to deal with a person in a way which it could previously have done, a Detention and Training Order is made with respect to an individual of 18 or over, that person will be treated as if s/he had been sentenced to a Young Offender Institution for the same term [s.106 PCCSA 2000)].

NB. The court imposing the second sentence may impose it immediately (if the offender has been released from the custodial part of the first sentence) or partly concurrent or consecutive to the custodial part of the existing sentence if s/he has not been released. The regime for release etc will be that applicable to the later sentence.

Remands & Committals

- Where a court remands a child/young person
  charged with or convicted of 1 or more offences or
  commits her/him for trial or sentence and s/he is
  not released on bail:
  - The remand/committal will be to local authority
    accommodation (which the local authority is
    obliged to provide) [s.23 CYPA 1969 as
    substituted by s.60 CJA 1991]

- A court remanding a person to local authority
  accommodation must designate the local authority
  who are to receive her/him which will be:
  - For a 'looked after' child/young person, the
    local authority so doing
  - In any other case, the local authority in whose
    area it appears to the court s/he resides or
    where offence or one of the offences was
    committed [s.23(2) CYPA 1969 substituted by
    s.60 CJA 1991]

  *NB. It is lawful for any person acting on behalf of the
  designated authority to detain a person who has
  been remanded to local accommodation [s.23 (3)
  CYPA 1969 as substituted by s.60 CJA 1991].
  s.132(2) CJPA 2001 inserts s.23AA into CYPA 1969
  setting out criteria and arrangements for electronic
  monitoring of 12–16 year olds remanded to local
  authority accommodation.*

Remand & Committals to Secure Accommodation

- There are two versions of s.23 CYPA 1969 as amended by the CDA 1998 which are relevant to remands and committals to custody.

- The principal version described immediately below deals with all juveniles aged 12–14, and 15 and 16 year old females. The modified one described thereafter deals with the particular provisions for specified 15 and 16 year old males.

All Juveniles 12–14 & Females Aged 15 & 16

- Subject to conditions described immediately below a court remanding a person to local authority accommodation may, after consultation with the designated authority require that authority to comply with a security requirement i.e. that the person in question be placed and kept in secure accommodation [s.23 (4) CYPA 1969 as substituted by s.60 CJA 1991 and amended by s.97 (1) CDA 1998].

- Criteria for the imposition of a security requirement are that the individual:
  - Is charged with or convicted of a violent or sexual offence or an offence punishable in the case of an adult with imprisonment for a term of 14 years more **or**
  - Is charged with or has been convicted of one or

more imprisonable offences which, together with any other imprisonable offences of which s/he has been convicted in any proceedings amount (or would amount if s/he were convicted of the offences with which s/he is charged) to a recent history of repeatedly committing imprisonable offences while remanded on bail or to local authority accommodation

- **And in addition,** the court is of the opinion, **after considering all the options** for the remand of the individual, that only a secure remand would be adequate either to protect the public from serious harm from her/him **or** to prevent the commission by her/him of imprisonable offences [s.23(5AA) CYPA 1969 as amended by s.130(3) CJPA 2001]

NB. Serious harm is defined in s.161 PCCSA 2000 in relation to sexual and violent offences as 'death or serious personal injury, whether physical or psychological, occasioned by further such offences committed by him'. It is not defined in relation to other offences.

A 'violent or sexual offence' is one listed in s.161 PCCSA 2000. 'Recent' and 'repeat' are not defined and are for the courts to determine.

- Where a court imposes a security requirement it must in open court:
    - State that it is of such opinion as cited in subsection 5AA and
    - Explain in ordinary language why it is of that

opinion (and a Magistrates' Court must record in the warrant of commitment and enter in the register its justification) [s.23(6) CYPA 1969 as substituted by s.60 CJA 1991]

▦ A court cannot impose a security requirement in respect of a child/young person who is not legally represented unless:

- S/he applied for legal aid and the application was refused on the ground it did not appear that her/his means were such as to require assistance or
- Having been informed of her/rights to apply for legal aid and had the opportunity to do so, s/he refused or failed to apply [s.23(5A) CYPA 1969 as inserted by s.97(3) CDA 1998]

Alternative Provision for 15 or 16 Year Old Males [s.98 CDA 1998]

▦ Pending the provision of sufficient secure accommodation, priority will be given to 15 and 16 year old boys at risk of remand to a remand centre or prison and who meet the definition of 'vulnerability' in s.23 (5) CYPA 1969 as substituted by s.98(3) CDA 1998 and described below.

▦ A court **must** remand to local authority accommodation and require the boy to be placed in secure accommodation if, after consultation with a social worker of a local authority, probation officer or member of a YOT, a court declares his offending behaviour satisfies the criteria of s.23(5) CYPA 1969 as substituted by s.130(2) CJPA 2001 i.e. he is charged with or has been convicted of:

- A violent or sexual offence or an offence punishable in the case of an adult with imprisonment for a term of 14 years or more, **or**
- One or more imprisonable offences which, together with any other imprisonable offences of which s/he has been convicted in any proceedings amount (or would amount if s/he were convicted of the offences with which s/he is charged) to a recent history of repeatedly committing imprisonable offences while remanded on bail or to local authority accommodation
- **And in addition,** the court is of the opinion, **after considering all the options** for the remand of the individual, that only remanding him to a remand centre or prison or to local authority accommodation with a requirement that he be placed and kept in secure accommodation, would be adequate either to protect the public from serious harm from her/him **or** to prevent the commission by her/him of imprisonable offences [s.23(5AA) CYPA 1969 as substituted by s.130(6) CJPA 2001]
- **And** the court further declares him to be a person to whom s.23(5A) as substituted applies ie. is of the opinion that by reason of his physical or emotional immaturity or propensity to harm himself, it would be undesirable for him

to be remanded to a remand centre or prison
and it has been notified that secure
accommodation is available [s.23(4)(a) CYPA
1969 as substituted by s.98(3) CDA 1998].

- Otherwise it will remand him to a prison [s.23 (4) (c)
CYPA 1969 as substituted by s.98 (3) CDA 1998].

- A court cannot declare that the boy's offending
behaviour satisfies the criteria of s.23 (5) CYPA 1969
unless he is either legally represented, or applied for
legal aid and was refused on the ground that it did
not appear his means justified it, or having been
informed of his right to apply for legal aid and had
the opportunity to do so he refused or failed to
apply [s.23 (4A) CYPA 1969 as substituted by s.98
(3) CDA 1998].

Miscellaneous Provisions

Disclosure of Information [s.115 CDA 1998]

- This section provides explicit authority for the following organisations to disclose information to police, probation or health authority or to persons acting on their behalf so long as such disclosure is necessary or expedient for the purposes of this Act:
  - Chief officer of police for a police area in England Wales or Scotland or a police authority within the meaning of s.10191) Police Act 1996
  - In relation to England, a county or district council, a London borough or city of London
  - In relation to Walkes, a county or county borough council
  - In relqtion to Scotland, a council constituted under s.2 Local Government etc (Scotland) Act 1994
  - A probation committee in England and Wales
  - A health authority/PCT

Sentencing Advisory Panel [s.81 CDA 1998]

- A new Sentencing Advisory Panel is established to provide advice on sentencing to the Court of Appeal.

- The Panel (members of which will be appointed by the Lord Chancellor) must be informed when the Court produces guidelines and then provide advice, consulting with other interested parties.

- The Panel may also propose that the Court frame or revise guidelines if it considers this necessary or is directed to do so by the Home Secretary.

Appendix 1: CAE Publications

■ Personal Guides:
  - Children Act 1989 in the Context of the Human Rights Act 1998
  - Childminding and Day Care (England)
  - Child Protection
  - Residential Care of Children
  - Fostering
  - 'How Old Do I Have To Be…?' (simple guide to the rights and responsibilities of 0–21 year olds)
  - Domestic Violence – (Part IV Family Law Act 1996 & Protection from Harassment Act 1997)
  - Looking After Children: Good Parenting, Good Outcomes (DH LAC System)
  - Crime and Disorder Act 1998
  - Sexual Offences Act 2003
  - Anti Social Behaviour

All available from: 103 Mayfield Road, South Croydon, Surrey CR2 0BH tel: 020 8651 0554 fax: 020 8405 8483 email: childact@dial.pipex.com

www.caeuk.org

Discounts for orders of 50 or more of any one title